Theresa Marie Lewis |

HOPE.

Matthew: "I'm proud of you because you keep surprising yourself.

You are amazing, you really are an inspiration".

- *No, my darling, it is You that is my inspiration.*
Thank you for standing by my side and never ending your love and support for me.
Even when I doubt myself, you always remind me to keep going.
Thank you for embracing me with all my trials, all my heartaches, all my pain.
You didn't run away. Instead you ran towards me with open arms.

I love you and our beautiful human creations endlessly!

Thank you, all those beautiful souls who continue to write. Keep pushing, keep emoting!

Artists are humans too!

Her.

Her vision is always 20/20.
She sees the good in everything.
Seeing the world for what it is and still, she doesn't stop.
Corruption. Deceit. Lies.
Used as credit by their faithful servants.
She is a Bystander to the wicked.
She has witnessed the evil,
She remains untouched.
She remains **confident**.

Waking each morning with a clear vision,
She knows the way.
Seeing. Believing. Following
Occurs immediately after crossing her path.
She **educates** others on acceptance.
She is a wonder.

Stepping into a new year,
She doesn't need a resolution.
She is the solution.
Omitting the lies that said she wasn't ready,
She patiently awaits her time.
She is worth it.
She is **majestic**.

Brown eyes, blue skies.
She sees a new beginning.
Love. Connection. Embrace.
She is amazed at the hues of her skin.
Seeing nothing more than beauty,
She is marvelous.
She is **Black**.

Eyes closing shut
She counts her blessings.
Squeezing the one that matters the most,
She is a fighter.

She is strong.

Mahogany.

I am a beautiful shade of Melanin.
To you, I will be called Beautiful.
To me, I will be known as graceful.
To the world, I will be looked at as royalty.

I am a perfectly crafted mahogany!
I have been created by the hands of God.
I am bathed in a tub filled of lavender.
My clothes are woven by the angels.

I am a beautiful shade of Blackness!
The streets are stained by my ancestors.
My feet will know no sorrow
For by the sweat on their backs I am renewed.

I am a perfectly created woman.
I know **WHO** I am and **WHAT** I am meant to be.
To you I will be called a queen.
To the world I am

Tee.

Tee.

Who is that woman that I see?
She walks around so gracefully.
Holding her head ever so high
I watch her as she passes by.

I must know that woman over there
Her confidence is magnetic,
I can't help but stare.
I want to brush by her,
In hopes that she'll care
That I have been staring,
Over here.

I want to ask her for her name,
That small piece of her I must claim.
It will change my life just to know,
How she lives her life with such a glow.
I'll catch up to her so we can talk
I hope she won't mind me joining her walk.
I need to tap into her grace
To be mesmerized by her face.

I need the courage to talk to that queen
To be stunned by what I've seen.
My heart already is beating fast
Because that queen has so much class.
To think she might notice me,
I'll say my name is "**Tee**".

As she moved closer, I saw no stranger,
And my staring held no danger.
That woman I wanted to know
Looked at me and said "*hello*".
Getting closer made things clearer
That the whole time she held a mirror.
The last thing I heard her say was,

"I'm happy that you looked my way".

Being confident didn't come easy for me. For many years, I admired the strength and dignity of strong, beautiful Black women. Empowered women empower women. One thing I believe I have in common with the leaders of yesterday is the vision to inspire others to enter tomorrow with strength and dignity. Continue to uplift each other as you were once uplifted.

Strong, Black, and Gifted.

To be young, **BLACK**, and gifted.
To be everything they wanted to be,
but couldn't.
Everything we are destined to be
And are.
To be proud of the **melanin** that runs through our veins.

Thank you, my ancestors.
Thank you, Nina Simone for introducing me to those
Four Women.
Each one imprinting their message in soul:
>*"Beautiful is the only 'B' word I will be called".*

Thank you, Billy Holiday for finding the rhythm
For my blues.
Thank you, Rosa Park for sitting still so I know where to stand.
Thank you, Harriet Tubman for running through the night so I can walk
Proudly through the day.

>*Walking through life now doesn't seem as impossible, all the honor to you.*

Yellow Hue.

There is something majestic about the yellow hue
Radiating from you and
Surrounding me.
There is something graceful about the way you sway
That makes me want to
Join you.
There is something beautiful about the way you
Stand out I wish
I can imitate.
There is something powerful about the life you
Bring that allows me to
Search for more.
I'm searching for the right way to ask you
Why you chose me.
You chose me.
There is something peaceful about being able to see you.
I see you.

And now I stand still while your light shines on me.

Exposed.

I've searched my whole life for this *feeling*.
A *feeling* I knew I would sacrifice *everything* for.
Everything I have experienced led to this *moment*.
A *moment* I knew would last a *lifetime*.
A *lifetime* of fully embracing all aspects of this *will*.
A *will* I refuse to abandon after the *fire* almost destroyed me.
The *fire* that burned through my bones but couldn't penetrate
My *soul*.
My *soul* has remained resilient throughout these *trials*.
These *trials* kicked me in the chest and tried to puncture
My *heart*.
But my *heart* was *resistant*.
My *resistance* allowed me to remain *still*.

Still, **I rise** *above* all the hatred thrown my way.
Above all, I accept this feeling
I thought I would *never* know.
I *never* knew I was *capable* of opening up this
side of me.
Now I am *capable* of shedding my *dead skin*.
The *dead skin* that I carried all these *years* thinking
It would still fit.
Years it took for me to search for this feeling.

And now I am bare.

Barely *bothered*.
Bothered by the thought that I almost didn't *find* it.
Find this feeling that leaves me *exposed*.
Exposed only to those who are ready to *release*.
Release the *thoughts* that said I am less than.
Thoughts of dignity that now occupy my *mind*.
My *mind* that is elated to find this feeling

I searched my whole life for.

Still, I March.

This countryside is the only side that is holding us back.
We live in a society that is not ready to hear
But is forced to listen.
I take a stroll on the right side of change.
I wear my skin unapologetically Black.
Making sure I step out when the sun is at its peak.
Damn, I should've put on sunscreen.
Sun frying up my skin extra crispy.
It's about time I made this journey!

Unlike you, I am not ashamed of my skin's hue.
I own who I am, and I love standing out.
Even when you look at me and roll your eyes, **still I march**.
Even when you are trained to hate me,
I will not look down.

You hold no weight over my life because
The weight has already been carried by my ancestors.
From their wombs they carried the burden
For me to be birthed anew.
Trying to push me off the path as if I didn't belong.
These are our streets.
My people paved them.
Mixing the cement with the sweat from their backs,
We own 100% royalty.

These steps are centuries in the making.
Listening to the drums of my ancestors' heartbeats,
They pound my way through.
Hearing the songs of their cries
they yell to me,
"KEEP MARCHING MY DAUGHTER"!
Pressing through the only way I know how,
Each step is long overdue.

Marching on the path ahead of me
It is the end of *this* world.
The world you created hoping my people won't get up.
But we rise!
Knocking the dirt off our back,
WE get up.
The same dirt you used to throw at my ancestors,
Falls right off.
We are not meant to oppressed.
I am not meant to stay still,
So instead, **I march.**
Marching on to yonder past the devil's creek
I must keep going.

2020 brings a lot of things into the forefront, including racism and cultural insensitivity. If I had only one wish to live, I will use it on safeguarding and protecting my children from the hatred and wickedness of society. Reality is, no matter how secure my shield over them is, the world will still see them as Black boys and to many, that would not be enough.

I pray above all, I instill in them the lesson to love themselves despite whether others love them. Without self-love, they risk walking through this world as an imposture.

Dear Boys,

Dear boys,
I need you to remember it is not how you look
But who you look like that would make the difference.
They will **test** you.
They will **trick** you.
They will **try** you.
They will tell you all the **wrong** things I never would.
They will **doubt** my love for you.
They will **disapprove** my protection of you
They will **disbelieve** the pain I bore for you.
They will attempt to **erase** the sacrifices I made for you.

Sweet caramel boys,
It's important you remember who you are,
Not what you are!
This will make all the difference.
You are **not** the monsters that lurk in the dark
Waiting for the next victim.
You are **not** scrapped meat thrown to the
wolves as prey to satisfy their needs.
You **are** the calm that shields us before their storm.
You **are** the peaceful air that breezes through on a warm summer day.
You are **majestic**.
You are **Black** children.

The sun glazed over your beautiful skins long enough to leave a lasting
glow.
Hold on to this glow.
For they want to destroy it.
They will lie to you.
They will force your eyes shut
Hoping to convince you the glow was never there,
Only to realize they hate you for having it.
Keep your bright brown eyes open.
Keep watching out for them.

Watch out for the ones who smile to your faces and talk to your back.
Either they talk to your faces or
You smile at their back.
Those conversations need to be one way.

Pay less attention to what they say and more to how they say.
The message may be innocent, but the messenger has a track record.
Stay clear of it.
Keep your hands clean from the trash they serve you because
Trash belongs in the garbage,
Not in your head.

Most importantly my beautiful boys,
Remember it's not who you are now
but what you will become that is the most
Threatening to them.

Today you are **Black children**.
Tomorrow you will be **Black kings**.

And every king must defend their throne.

Black and White.

To whom it may concern (a.k.a. YOU),

You're a racist!

You have no idea what it's like to be "*black*",
To have your entire existence scrutinized by the world.
To have been forced on that ship!
Your imagination won't go far enough to witness
the plight my people experience,

DAILY.

How could you?
You're not one of us!
Do you know the struggle we go through just to fit in?
America mocks our skin while you prance around the streets

Invincible.

We had no choice in those fields!
The sun burned through us while you safely sipped your freshly
made ice cold lemonade.
The sun highlighted your glow every time you stepped outside

I hate you.

I hate everything you represent.
I hate your entire existence.
It's not fair you are favored.
It's not right Society pardons you just because your head is covered with
soft curls.
Panic never paralyzes you when the sight of water threatens to destroy
your perm, your weave, your wig.
No, you don't need any of those to rest on top of your head praying it will
fix the mistake that is called,

Your hair.

You even have water on your side.
We are tired of investing all we have on correcting ourselves and all you
do is wake up.

God must have been mad at us.
You open your mouth and everyone listens to you.
People actually stop what they're doing to be
serenade by your voice.
What makes you so special?
We deserve more

NOT YOU!

We don't have your certified papers or your fancy clothes but fuck it!
Who needs that anyway?
What are you anyway, since clearly you're not a part of us.
It's obvious

You're not Black

Oh wait... you must be white mixed with something else.
You must be that breed the owners wanted a piece of.
That uppity mix.
And your name is Theresa Marie?
Yeah, that just proves our point.

Since you're not with us, you are against us.
I hope you fall off that bougie ass high horse you arrived on.
Disrespectful submitted,

Your typical,

"Black person".

*My brothers, you do not have to carry the weight of the world on your shoulders anymore. Sooner or later, the load will be unbearable, and it will all slip away. Do not lose yourself in someone else's perception of who you are. Life is too short to live up to the expectations of others. Live for yourself. Live for your families. Live for the **HOPE** of a world that will accept you as who you are, Kings.*

Colored Man.

I am a "Colored" man.
Well, that's who they say I am.
They trampled me down with their Klan.
Breaking my legs so I won't stand.

My eyes once had pride.
My community used me as a guide.
But now my identity has died.
And my skin is fried.

"YOU'RE JUST A COLORED MAN",
They say.
As they cut me up and used me as prey.
Smoking my soul and dumping it in an ashtray.
Leaving the rest of me to decay.

In my lifespan
I'll never be a Black Man
Since all they planned

Was for me to be a Colored Man.

Black Man.

I am a Black man.
I say it, believe it, accept it,
To make my stand.
I hold my shoulders wide.
For I have nothing to hide.
I wear my hair in a high tide.

I am a Black man.
I rock with my own Klan.
They all call me *Mr. Bogeyman.*
I make my own rules.
I use my skin as my best tool.
Don't bother me with your racial cesspool.

I am a Black man.
I'm my own best fan.
I'll always be proud

OF WHO I AM.

Caterpillars are not meant to fly; however, they are meant to develop into a higher sense of being. This greater purpose will bring them to new heights. Caterpillars are not meant to jump, however, they are meant to sacrifice their originate form in the **HOPE** *of becoming something beautiful.*

I once thought all I was meant to do in this was crawl, until my wings began to merge and before I knew it, I was transformed.

Transformation.

What happens to you when you reach the sky?
When at first you believed you were meant to die.
When life as you knew it, you lived on the ground.
And the feelings you had, could not be found.

What happens to you on your way up?
As you fly by all the Caterpillars who refuse to jump.
Who thought by denying you they would interrupt?
The butterfly you are destined for without any stumps.

What will happen to me as I look down?
At all the Caterpillars crawling around.
Knowing inside I will never see,
Why they tried so hard not to let me be.

This majestic creature that is free

Thanks to my transformation that is really me.

I Found Me.

I finally found my identity
It took so long for me.
I once gave up **hope** and struggled with
Who I wanted to be.

I finally found my identity
A woman the world must see.
My chains of self-hatred are broken
Finally, I am set free.

I finally found my identity
The one I have not known
It too great courage to open up
And let my beauty be shown.

I finally found my identity
It took so long for me.
But I'm glad I made this journey

Because I found ME.

Love is a beautiful thing. It validates all the insecurities one may have while supporting the **HOPE** *for a satisfying and richer life. I searched for unconditional love my whole life. The journey led me to many dead ends and detours, but the path eventually leads me back to you. My soul found yours when we were both in heaven. My eyes saw yours when we were children. My heart welcomed yours when we were both young adults. Loving you will always be my greatest accomplishment. Thank you, my love for standing by my side endlessly.*

Welcome into my Heart.

I love you.
Let me explain.
It feels like our souls have been connected long before our minds have.
I am comfortable around you,
I feel secure around you,
I am myself around you.

I cannot say the same for many people.
No, to most people I am the complete opposite.
Most people need to undergo an investigation before I expose my them to
my core.
Most people must pass the toughest battle
To receive a small fragment of
Theresa Marie.

But not you.
With you,
I knew I could trust you the first moment I laid eyes on you.
With you,
Everything seemed natural.
With you,
I knew I had a support system.
To know me is to know why loyalty is an
Essential part of my life.

When I connect with someone,
I give my all.
I hand over my heart,
    My emotions,
        My mind and all I ask in return is
            Equality.
               Treat me the same way you treat yourself.
               Care for me the same way you care for yourself.
               Love me the same way you love yourself.
               Once I know we are at that level,
               You will gain my *love*
               A love that I will cherish until the day I die.

Welcome into my heart.

My darling,

I look into your eyes and

Catch a reflection of my soul.

Finally, I found my match.

My darling,

Your caught the attention of the hairs on the back of my neck

As you gently kissed my forehead

Whispering, *"I love you"*.

And with that,

My heart began to beat.

Matthew G. Lewis.

My life has been changed by you.
Accepting my fate, I am forever joined to you.
Trusting you with each fragment of my heart,
This is why I love you.
Happiness is the continuation of the moments we share together.
Everything I do is for us.
Walking down our aisle was my greatest accomplishment.

Granting your heart's desire is my purpose.

Loving you is my life's purpose.
Enchanting you is my highest priority.
Who I am today is a reflection of what you mean to me.
I commit myself to you.
Sincerely yours,

Now and forevermore.

Happiness.

Happiness rest in the moments
You whisper in my ear causing
My teeth to feast off my bottom lip.

Happiness rest in the moments
You kiss my neck soft enough
For me to scream for more yet,
Hard enough for **X** to mark it's spot.

Happiness rest in the moments
I surrender to you.
In the moments I let it all flow,

For you.

Love Haiku.

My heart skipped a beat
You became my sweet heartbeat

My heart is now complete.

Something Like a Love Story.

I've been fucked all my life in ways I never really enjoyed.
My body is numb to the penetration.
My senses recognize the stench quickly approaching long before it came.
I don't want to be fucked by you.

Love me instead.

Serenade me while I marinade in the sweet melody of your words.
Seduce me with the idea that I am the greatest thing since life's bread.
Tease me with the thought that there will never be another like me.

Embrace me.

Let the juice flow down my oyster quench your thirst
Leaving my purest pearl as your prize possession.
Use me as your prize possession.
Let me claim all your prize as my possession.

Caress me.

Hold me tight.

Dear December 31, 2019, I'm sorry. I should have respected you more. I should have stopped to smell your roses. I should have realized all you needed was for me to be present, to acknowledge, to accept that the blessings I was given could easily be taken away. What better teacher to teach that lesson than COVID-19? The real pandemic is the various worlds and roles merging into one. The real struggle is trying to process where this is a nightmare or reality. The real heartache is knowing I will not get you back. So 2019, you were indeed good to me. I see it now.

2020.

20/20 brought new vision but the lenses were foggy.

2020 brought new beginnings but we were not prepared for the end.

2020 brought its hindsight but ignorance was bliss.

Damn, I wish I had a reset button.

Nightmare.

I find myself waking up each night
To feel your sweet lips kiss me goodnight
But the night betrays me with a fight.
So instead I turned off the lights.

Must've been a bad dream.

Midnight

I heard a knock at my door at 12 a.m.
I cracked it open to get a better look.
Struggling to see you in the dim light,
You stood still as you watched me.
Wavering in this dark room,

Finally, I am not alone.

Reboot.

2020 was supposed to bring me success
Instead all I have seen is death.
Without the peace of laying them to rest.
Has my faith registered for the ultimate test.

The doctor told me I had 20/20
Clearly, I don't.
Since nothing is straight anymore.
I may actually need corrective lenses.

People are hiding,
Children are whining,
Elders are dying and
Parents are crying.

And for what?

If that's what my vision brings that someone call
Sandra Bullock because
I'm ready for my tryouts.

Birdbox Sequel,

Staring, Tee.

Losing a child is one pain I do not wish on anyone. My child died in my stomach, others ma
pass in a car accident, hospital bed, their loved one's arms. The circumstances do not matte
as much as the void that will never be filled again. You were going to be my eldest. You wer
going to be my saving grace however, God had other plans. Instead, you were meant to teac
me the lesson that nothing is ever certain. There are no concrete plans. Life ends as quickly a
it begins. June 18, 2013, I found out your heartbeat stopped. June 23, 2013, the doctor
permanently removed you from me. I remember waking up from the anesthesia and crying t
the medical team how sorry I was that my body could not keep you and still am. You held n
place in my body however, you will forever hold a place in my heart.

Mommy will forever love you.

Lost Child.

I wish I held you.
I wish I knew what you would smell like.
I often think about who you would look like.
I kept your death hidden.
I refused to talk about you.
I didn't want to remember the moments you were inside me.
For months you were thriving, you were growing, you were living.
Until one day you were not.
One day you were taken from me.
One day you were gone.
One day you were dead and there was absolutely nothing I could do to
change that.
But you changed me.
When you died, I was born.
Your death birthed a deeper appreciation for life.
Because of you, I learned what it meant to have a mother's love.

Because of you I knew I would cherish every moment I shared with your
brothers.
Because of you I knew how to give my all and expect nothing in return.
Because of you I had to accept that I would never hear your voice.
I am sorry my body rejected you.
I am sorry my heart had to mourn you.
I am sorry my mind had to create false ideas of who you would be.
I am sorry your brothers would never get the chance to meet you, laugh with
you, play with you, love you.
I am sorry you never had the opportunity to listen to your father sing,
To have him serenade you with his music.
I am sorry your life ended too soon, before you were given the chance to
shine.

Now all you do is shine from heaven.
Now all you do is wipe away my tears as I cry myself to sleep.
Now all you do is watch over us and keep us safe.
Now all you do is whisper "I love you too mommy" to my soul.
My soul that is longing to be near yours.
You were my child.
You were the air I breathe in.
You were my first.

Now?

Now you are a memory of a life that quickly ended before it had the
chance to start.
Now you are the silent voice of my family, a family that never knew you.
Now you are a light that has been put out.
Now you are the day that has become night.
Now you are a piece of me that will forever be missed.
Now you are my child. A child that I lost.

Forgive me my love so that I may one day forgive myself.

Death is a nature part of life. We live to die so one day; our memories could inspire others to **HOPE** *for more.* **Hope** *for a brighter future.* **Hope** *for the end of jealousy, corruption, and ill-will. That is the mark I want to leave on this earth. For those to know me as the person who kept marching, despite the trials. Life is not easy. People would not always like you. Friends may turn their backs on you & family may seclude you. It can feel suffocating at first. It will not be easy to cope with. You may even ask yourself "why you?". "What have you done to deserve this pain?". Sadly, the answer is as simple as you were born to stand out. Yes, it can get lonely at the top but once you are up there, the tranquility that engulfs you is one you would have never known had you sacrifice the need to be loved by others for the desire to be loved by yourself. Keep going.*

Death.

My hope for when I die is for pieces of my soul
Too be planted in the hearts
Of all the lives I touched.
All those smiles I handed out free of charge,
Free of expectations that I should receive one back.
Free of the worry that I had to wear one all the time
To mask my pain.

When I die,
I want my spirit to fill the gaps where
Resentment laid.
The spirit of resiliency that I would not be knocked down.
The satisfaction of knowing that I was much stronger
Then they **HOPE** *I was.*

When I die,
I want everyone to surround me
Remembering me as a person who loved
Above all.
I want my memory to fly like birds in the sky
And in those moments,
I want everyone to know that I will live with

them forever.

Dearly Beloved.

Dearly beloved,
I come before you this evening in a time of deep sorrow.
I stand before you in remembrance of a voided memory.
I am here to talk about the memory that I loss.
Before we begin,
    My fellow poets,
        Please join me in a moment of silence
           As we allow ourselves to think back on that time when,
        I died.

                        Thank you.

Now, let's start from how it happened because this death
Did not happen today.
No, it happened the first moment you laid eyes on me
Solidifying in your heart that I will never be
"Good enough".
It happened the moment I dived into your World
Knowing I couldn't swim yet watching you
Puncture the only life jacket I could have used.
I was left thinking,
    Feeling,
        Believing,
           I would survive.
           BUT,
              What survived was your will to kill me.

                      And you did.

I was dying in the middle of that room with your hands clasped
Around my neck refusing to release me.
You made sure I could not scream out for help as you
Continued to tighten your grip.
The first part that faded was my heart.
    The heart that was shattered by you.
        And of course, that wasn't enough for you.
        No, you had to continue with my murder.

                    You drugged me.

You fed me the substance of false **HOPE** knowing
I had an addiction.
You watched me scrambling for more while at the same time
restricting me from getting my next fix.
You mocked me as my body went
through withdrawals begging for it to stop.
I was convulsing.
    I was shaking.
        I was hallucinating
           And you didn't care.

What's the simplest way to kill an addict?
> You give them the drug.
>> You knew I would keep coming back for more.

And I did.

I ran to you for what felt like miles only to realize I was traveling in circles.
The harder I ran the tighter the circles became until they started closing in
on me.
> My mind struggled to get out,
>> All you did was watch.
>>> Even with your haunting looks
>>>> I held on.

I held on to your empty promises,
> Your false hope,
>> Your fleeting memory.
>>> I held onto it all until you took your final blow.

You left.

You disappeared from my memory
Leaving me with a void.
A voided memory of us that I now have to bury forever.
> Goodbye to the possibility that we could have been amazing.
>> But we weren't since you killed me before I was able to live.

Now I stand before you,
> My fellow poets,
>> In the abstinence of hope
>>> Finally sealing the casket shut.
>>>> Rest in Peace my innocence,

Gone and already forgotten.

Purification.

I threw a rope down into the dark abyss
Praying I would find the strength to rescue myself.
"Spend time with family",
      "Reconnect with old friends",
            They say,
                  Whoever *"**they**"* are.

Sure, that's the solution.
It's obvious I completely forgotten
      How to be a part of this family,
          How to be an old friend.
             How to just be **me**.
Sarcasm intended.

"JUST BE"
Is a familiar demand.
I have done it so well
      I know how we go about life
          Without you reminding me what to do.

In case I do forget,
You will send a friendly reminder that
I've failed at breaking this cycle,
      Yet again.
        Shucks.

Seems like I have some homework to do.

What is the function of your hatred towards me?
Self-fulling,
      Attention,
          Escape?

You exposed me,
      Opened me,
          Carved me out.
Made my soul bleed
Replacing what was untainted with
What is tarnished.
      Gone.
         Ouch.
That sucks.

I need to be purified.
Come out of denial about my feelings,
Just be…
      Honest….
        Raw…

Taking a hard look at why I feel the way I do,
Where your hatred came from,
I need to heal front this hurt inside me.
My whole body hurts.
     My head hurts.
          My heart hurts.

I need to cleanse myself...
     And it starts now.

With you.

Most young adults spend their college years exploring the world, exploring each other, exploring life's boundaries. I, on the other hand, spent my college years exploring myself. That exploration unfortunately ended in one night I will spend my remaining years trying to erase. That night I will forever blame myself for not finding my inner strength sooner. If only I was found sooner. If only I walked down a different hallway. If only I didn't have to remix the lyrics to "99 bottles of beer in your cup".

99 Bananas.

99 bananas of liquor in your cup
99 bananas of liquor,
Drink one down, pass it around
99 bananas of liquor in your cup.

Oh wait, is that how the song goes?
I don't think so.
Let's try this again.

We put 99 bananas of liquor in her cup
99 bananas of liquor,
Strip her down, pass her around
She has 99 bananas of liquor in her....
amongst other ingredients...
But
Don't tell.

The rotten banana's aroma has a residue similar to a hollow ant's body
after sitting too long under a magnifying glass.
There's no escape from the stench that is leaves on my pores.
One drop on my tongue closes my throat as my body goes into shock.
The yellow hue serves as a cataract over my eyes.

It took 99 bananas to make me lose myself.
The 99th banana transported me to an alternate reality where I was paralyzed
and they were invigorated.
I wish I had one more or one less banana.
One less banana may have kept me awake.
One more banana may have kept me strong.
The right amount of bananas could have kept me in control.
But it didn't.
I was not in control because I didn't have enough bananas.
God, I hate bananas.

I was drugged by 99 bananas of liquor in my cup
99 bananas of liquor,
I drunk one down was raped all around
By 99 bananas of liquor and all.

Positive Self-Talk.

"I was raped", is not my story.
I am not in a category
My scars are my glory.
Accepting me, is mandatory.

I am not a victim.
I am not in a system.
My experience is my wisdom
"I am a survivor", is my dictum.

I am not damaged.
My world is not ravaged.
My sanity is now managed.
My soul has been bandaged.

That night, I took.
Back from that crook.
I re-wrote my life's book

I am stronger than I look.

I would not do myself justice if I did not admit this crown can be heavy at times. Even the most powerful of birds need to rest as I too, need to rest. Being broken down and tired once drained me. Looking up at the mountaintop, I once struggled to rise. My heart mourned. My soul ached. It was getting heard to breathe carrying it all alone. There were days all I did was cry.

Crying is not a sign of weakness. It is a sign of endurance. It is a sign of **HOPE.** *Once the tears dry, I will rise.*

When Eagles Cry.

I can't always be strong.
The burden to soar above it all is heavy.
My wings are bruised from your weight.
I struggled to carry your baggage.

The sky was supposed to be the limit.
You have robbed me from my limit.
Now all I see is the ground.

The ground has become my hiding place.
My feet have been permanently planted in the shadow of what once was.
My lungs no longer breathe in the remedy of **hope**.

My eyes have been perched on the memory of us.
The wind is unable to dry the tears flowing down my face.
My power has ceased.

My spirit has abandoned me.

This is what happens when eagles cry.

Negative Self- Talk.

I don't see what they see.
Why be who they expect me to be?
So many demands placed on me.
Was I truly ever free?

I'll never be good enough.
Barely getting through this dirt trough.
Why is my life always so tough?
No one else understands my stuff?

Everything I touch, I screw up.
Every relationship I had, I blew up.
I don't know how to clean up,
So instead I will cover up.

Why do I feel this way?
Sliced up like a piece of filet.
I look outside and it all seems so gray.
Even if there's someone to talk to, what do I say?

If only I was worth it,
I would not want to quit.
How I feel is not what my mouth admit.
Because life is not a simple equation where everything must fit.

But it doesn't have to be this way,
Maybe I should kneel down and pray.
So my soul wouldn't have to stray,
And this struggle would go away.

To give room for HOPE to stay.

Safe Space.

People always say poetry is a safe space.
Folks talk about all types of shit from boyfriends,
To girlfriends,
To the baby daddy of your
Best friend.

All the raunchy lines
Raw vines all laid out there.
Poets bleed their hearts out all in the name of self-expression.
How authentically poetic is that?

You all inspire me so
Here goes...
I'm in an abusive relationship.

No punch line,
No hidden hooks.
It's all right there.

I'm tormented daily.
Fucking with my head so it can have control over
me.
Fucking up my body so it can control the maintenance I
need.

I been in this shit for too long,
Loving myself,
Hating myself,
Not having a sense of self,
All for an image.

Flying so high on my good days you couldn't tell me shit
But on my bad days?
All I felt was empty.
Demanding me to submit every waking
Moments of the day.

"Eat this,
Sneak that,
Hide this,
Binge that".

It was just a game.
Whether I'm binging or restricting,
It's the same storyline,
"I'm not strong enough".

I hate losing the battle every night.
I hate looking like I'm trying out for the 2021 Olympics
JUST TO PUT JEANS ON!

All those years of hard work erased because
I can't control my fucking
EMOTIONS.

How sad is that!

I'm in an abusive relationship with what I thought was
Food
Only to realize it's with myself.

As the saying goes,
"Only the strong survive",
But in my case,

I'm barely even doing that.

Addiction.

All I wanted was acceptance
Yet in return I receive rejection.
I wish I could say the pain lessens with age
However, the only thing that lessens was
My ability to move on.

The part that hurt the most was the guilt I felt
When I broke free from this toxic web
Knowing they were still entwined.
The dosage I was prescribed was effective at keeping
Me hooked.

I've tried detox before.
I've hosted my own intervention.
But I am still struggling with this addiction.
So Here goes....

"Hello, this is my first time at a meeting.
My name is Theresa Marie.
I am addicted to **HOPE**".

"WELCOME THERESA MARIE".

*Disclaimer: People will use and manipulate you if you let them. Do not do it. Trust me, it's n
worth it. I had to learn that lesson the hard way. I had to teach myself to walk away, let g
give up. Surrendering doesn't mean they won; it just means you chose you first. I had
surrender the desire to conform, bend over backwards. I chose to be mentally healthy. I chos
to be happy. I chose me.*

Next Fix.

I recovered from this addiction
When you relapsed on my addiction.
You used me for your high
Forcing me to say goodbye.
The fix wasn't strong enough.
   Thank God.

Usually we're 70% water and
30% fucked up.
But you?
You are 30% water and 70% fucked up.
   How's that shit for biology?

Your energy became my enemy.
And now I'm drained.
One look at you and
   I'm triggered.

Triggered by all the moments I spent
Wanting to save you.
But the saving was completed by my mind drive.
   Thanks!

Thank you for reminding me I'm not God.
Thank you for forcing me to leave.

Thank you for proving me wrong.

*When **there's a** way, there is **Theresa**. Some people would not notice the significance in that sentence but it's okay, I do. I had an awakening the day I choose me. The flame in my eyes grew brighter and stronger. I grew stronger. Being in an intimate partner violent relationship almost killed me, both figuratively and literally. "He" threatened to take my breathe away if I ever left him. I did. I left that relationship so that I could live.*

Living is exactly what I intend to do. With every ounce in me to do so, I will live.

Birthday.

So today is my birthday.
      Hip hip hooray!
Only thing is my hip and hip is not shouting hooray!
HA!
Neither is my back but whose keeping score?
No,
My back started hurting way before I entered the 30 and up club.
My back has been hurting since I allowed you to put all your shit on it.
My back has been hurting ever since I had to carry,
Not only my baggage,
      But yours,
            Theirs, and
                  Everyone else around me.
My back has been hurting ever since you got the idea
In your head that you can walk on me like a
      Dirty dog
            Stomping on its filthy mat.

                  Guess what?
My back is hosting a parade!
The lineups are my feet that are
Tired of walking on egg shells around your selfish ass!
My shins that are burning from holding
It together so you won't kick into them as if they matter.
Next up are my knees,
Buckling with exhaustion because they want so badly
To bend but their pride refuses to let them
      Go down that way
            No pun intended.

Let's not forget these thighs that have been
Bruised and banged,
      Scratched and punched while you had your way with me.
           These thighs that are thick to their core yet fragile
               When you toss them on your floor.
In unison the parade shouts out,

"GET YOUR ASS UP.
GET IT TOGETHER,
SHOW THEM WHO YOU ARE!"

My back's parade does not march alone.
No, they have my shoulders that guards them from you.
YOU, you irrelevant piece of shit.
These shoulders?
They stand their ground!
Silly of you to think you would
ever knock them down!

If you thought that was nothing,
Just wait 'til you meet my arms!
  You really thought you could yank me,
    Pull me,
      Swing me any kind of way?
I feel bad for you if these go up.
But no,
I will save you the embarrassment,
The shocked disbelief of realizing that with these arms
Comes my hands.

Unlike you,
  I won't use my hands to slap you,
    Punch you,
      Pinch you.
But don't get it twisted.
These hands WILL defend themselves.

And you actually thought you had all of me.
You had your hands wrapped around my neck.
Squeezing it tight hoping it would crack.
But you made 1 mistake.
       You let go.
You
  Let go.
And with that release all the blood started to
Flow back to my head.
  This head you tried so hard to empty out.
    This head you thought was hollow.
      But you made 1 mistake...
       You forgot that today is my birthday.
And on my birthday,
I refuse to be used as your pawn.
I will not lay flat under dirty ass motherfucking shit infested boot.
Not on my birthday!
Today is my birthday and my gift to myself is,

LIFE.
Poderosa.

I had a dream you killed me,
But I was still alive.
You shot me,
But I was still whole.
You collapsed my lungs,
But I was still breathing.
You removed my soul and left my body to rot.

But why?

Why am I allowing you to take control over me?
I had a purpose.
I had a vision for my life but that wasn't good enough for you.
No, instead you had to be the center of attention.
Instead you had to steal my shine.

Why did my independence abandon me when I need it the most?
I was standing on my own.
I didn't need you to direct my path,
But I did want your support while I was on my way.

I needed you by my side.

Instead you separated yourself from me.
Why did my ego restrict me from **hoping** for the best?
This ego that was once confident and unbothered.
This ego that pushed past the barriers.
Instead you bruised my ego.

Why did I forget who I was?

I was someone,
I impacted lives,
I utilized my discernment,
Instead, you doubted me
Instead, I doubt myself.

Now what does that leave

If not the temptation to fall in your traps and
Reminders that I once rose above them.
You see,
I had that dream that you killed me,

But I woke up.

It felt like you had control over me,
But I am not powerless.

You might've thought I was dependent,
But I am self-sufficient.

You were convinced I wasn't esteemed,
But you failed to recognize the
                                    Love
I have for myself.
You wanted to erase the significance of my life,
But forgot to first erase the significance of my strength.
Now what does that leave other than the failure of your plans and the
elevation of my destiny?
Let me answer for you.
What it leaves is me,

                                    Poderosa.

Truth Is.

Truth is I'm tired.
Tired of holding my head up high,
Of running ahead to make sure the path is clear for you.
For using my blood, sweat and tears
To secure a life for you.
For arching my back to create a free ride for you.

Truth is I'm burned out.
Burned from holding the light long enough for you to see the way through.
Lighting up the sky so the world wouldn't see the dark in you.
Lighting up the best moments I thought I had with you.

Truth is I'm exhausted.
Exhausted from the commitment I made to try,
      Try,
           Try again.
I've been trying for too long to see the change in you.
The difference between me and the Little Engine that could is...
I couldn't.
I know I can't,
      I know I can't,
           I know I can't
             Keep believing in you.
Truth is I'm ready to give up.
I'm giving up on defending you.
I knew better.
I'm releasing all ideas of a better you.
Letting go of memories I created that told me I was happy.
I was never happy with you.

Truth is you are toxic to me.
You are the rock that should have never been discovered.
The rock that weighed me down.
You are my kryptonite.
The closer I got to you, the weaker I became no thanks you.

Truth is I've slowly been picking out shards of broken glass that pierced
my heart.
Picking off the best parts that made me.
Keeping the worst parts that tormented me.
Worst part was I was willing to die instead of you.

Truth is not anymore.
The only thing that will die is the control you had over me.
Now I will control how I am with you.
Truth is I will be true to me,

Not you.

Mental health matters, PERIOD.
Alongside of crying, seeking help is not a sign weakness. If anything, it is a sign of gr
strength. I will not pretend it is easy to say those three words: "I need help". But I do and y
know why? Because I am human. There are trained certified and licensed helpers. I sho
know because I am one of them. Yes, therapist needs therapy too.

Seek it.

Evacuation Plan.

How dare you enter my personal space
Without my knowledge and permission.
How dare you think your smooth words and
Slick tone was enough for me
to yield.
How dare you assume I have no will to stand my ground.
Was I supposed to let you enter my world unannounced?
Was I supposed to look the other way while you crept behind me
To get your fix.
Whose fixing me while I idly sit frozen waiting for my queue to exhale.

Exhale...

I'm waiting for my queue to release this shuddering breath.
I need to pace my breath in between the moments you whisper my name
and the moments I search for an escape.
I need to escape the awkwardness I feel reminding you
You are too close to my box.
The box you knocked down
Thinking it was okay to enter my world.
My world that was complacent prior to your entrance.
I need to expel you with the antigenic poisons you brought with you.
I need an evacuation plan for the next time you come near.

R-A-C-E:

Run.
    Abandon.
      Confine.
        Escape.

Go straight down the hallway,
Open the small black door and Enter.
Lock the door behind.
Do not turn on the light.

Take shallow breaths.
Stay still until it's time...

It's time.

Open your eyes and repeat.
Repeat the evacuation plan until it's no longer a plan.
Plan to memorize what I'll do when you enter
My personal space without

My knowledge and permission.

Abracadabra.

I can't say your name.
There's no pretending that I have the strength to.
I know my limits.
The power you have over me is greater than my power to overwrite you.
The magic markers I purchased were a rip off.

Crayola would be offended.

I'm embarrassed to admit I entered a dark alley to purchase them.
You see,
The dealer convinced me that these markers could erase
anything.
"*ANYTHING!?*" I asked.
"*Yes, anything!*
Just turn the tip, wave your hand and
BOOM!
Watch the magic begin".

Desperate I spent the last ounce of
hope
I had on the markers praying they
would work.

Only problem was Crayola was offended.
The magic didn't arrive
But my fear did.
Then again,

The markers were cheap.

Tainted Photograph.

You don't need to pretend anymore.
Feel free to remove the mask you wore for so long.
The image of us has already been altered

And away it you into the summer breeze

Along with the tainted photograph from yesterday.
We did a good job covering up the dust,
      Rips,
            Creases.
Ignoring those imperfections reappearing.

Struggling far too long to bring the beauty back,
The tainted photograph captured our darkest moment.
If you zoom in, you will have a view of our
Flawed relationship.
But no worries, I'll crop it later.
Filtering over our imperfections has never been easier.
With the right edits we'll have restoration

Yesterday, we preserved memories.
Today, we realize our photograph is tainted.
We will enter tomorrow damaged to one degree or another.
Fading,
      Staining,
            Shrinking will all leave their marks.

So, I will throw away our photograph returning to life.

Refusing to allow us to vast in the NOTHINGNESS of it all.

Shattered.

You shattered my heart.
You disrupted my very Existence.
I trusted you.
I confided in you.
I believed in you.

Yet what do I receive in return?
In my return I get nothing...
Abstinence.
The abstinence of **hope** that we'll return to
Before.

Hope that these feelings of resentment would dissipate.
Dissipate in the dark abyss,
Which is what is left of the heart
You shattered.

I used to think we were 2 peas in the pod
Until that pod developed a crack
And you were long gone.
I didn't mean to leave you behind.

I didn't expect you to walk in my tracks
I did expect you to embrace
your own.
But, how could you?

You were too busy devising your plan on
Ways to keep me under control.
You ruined the memory I wanted to have of us.

The "*us*" I now accept was never real.
Accept that you lost the opportunity to truly see me.
Now every time I see you,
I understand that I'm looking at nothing.

The Abstinence of nothing is a void.

A void that you created ever since you shattered my heart.

All Bets Are Off.

That moment you finally come to terms that the white gloves must come
off.
Correction,
That moment I need to accept that these gloves have been stained.
These gloves have been shredded to the thread that barely kept them on
my hands.
I'm afraid of taking these gloves off because of what they mean to me.
Correction,
I don't want to take off these gloves because of what they
represent to me.
Although stained and broken they guarded my hands.
They saved my skin each time a thorn pricked me.
Correction,
Each time a thorn pricked me, I blead.
The amount of blood that dripped from my clenched fist isn't what bothers
me the most.
It is the fact that I pretend that pain never happened.
It is the fact that I know that each thorn pierces,
      Punctures,
          Penetrates but
              Instead these gloves pretend.
                  Pretending for far too long that they were top notch quality.

These gloves,
Although drenched by the tears they unwillingly wiped away,
Almost kept me covered.
Broken by the whip that served 5 lashes across my arms,
These gloves tried too hard to protect me.
I was never really protected because of what they did to me.

Shielded from the commitment of embracing my bare hands,
These gloves suppressed me.
      They made my hands believe they needed them.
          Validating only the parts that serve them,
              These gloves fed me poison on a silver platter.
Reinforcing the idea that I needed them,
These gloves silenced my spirit.
I needed my gloves to survive.
Correction,
I wanted my gloves to sacrifice my hands from being bare.

I held on to the imagine that these gloves looked better on than off.
Drowning in the puddle of its own sweat,
My hands struggled to keep them on.
      Wobbling,
          Quivering,
              Bleeding,

My hands have exasperated all other means of control.

Driving down a one-way street these hands transport unconditional love.
Always ending at a dead end,
These gloves mock my independence.
    Questioning,
        Doubting,
            Submitting has always been the pattern.
          Silence,
            Surrender,
Fulfillment has always been the expectation.
Slowly peeling them off,
These hands wish the gloves won't stick.
Correction,
Snatching off the garments this pain will cease to exist.

And my hands will hurt no more.

Used, Abused, Numb.

I am punishing myself over what I know will never change.
I am exempt from having value in your world.
I am not a factor to be considered.
I am merely an insignificant vessel for which you use to dump your unwanted rubbish.
I am the dirt you refuse to leave on your doorstep because it paints a tainted picture that your life is flawed.
Simply, I do not matter to you.

I am used.
I am abused.
I am numb.

I am everything you never wanted yet always hated because I was there.
I am a slithering worm that torments the essence of a flower's beauty.
Or was it really a dried up weed?
I am a pestering ant declaring to destroy the perfectly planted picnic.
Or was it just a mirage?
I am a diseased fly threating to end the peaceful summer breeze.
Or was it a search for a cure?

I am used.
I am abused.
I am numb.

I am immune from the **hope** that things will get better.
The hope vaccine was unable to penetrate my soul.
I am immune from the desire to wish for change.
The courage medication couldn't stay in my system.
I am immune from the sacrifice of never leaving your side.
The loyalty prescription already expired.
I am immune from the commitment I thought you had for me.

I am used.
I am abused.
I am numb.

Love never was my cure.

Shadow.

You try so hard not to notice me,
I am not the focus of your attention.
I lost the opportunity to occupy your mind,
You barely detect that I'm here.
My only purpose is to verify that you exist.
You are the first thing everyone sees.
I have accepted that a long time ago.
I don't ask for much from you.
I know my fate;
I accept that my sole mission is to allow you to shine.
I only ask for acknowledgment.

Grant me the privilege to be talked about as well.
Allow me to shape myself into something beautiful for you.
Admit to the world that my existence matters.
Stop being so selfish!
Recognize that my presence is a factor.
Don't forget that before you came I was already here.
The world doesn't live in only daylight.

You think you can overpower me?
You really think I'm no longer important?
I suppose you think I have no feelings.
Perhaps you think I'm dead inside.
If it was your decision,
I'll be gone a long time ago.

I see the way you tilt your head,
Pretending you don't see me.
I know you constantly move around **hoping** that I'll disappear.
If only it was that easy to get rid of me.

Am I supposed to act like everything is okay?
Is this the moment where we recycle our movements
Pretending to be normal?
Don't get confused,
I CHOOSE to stay down.
I can get just as big as you are
Sometimes bigger.

Instead I stay loyal to you.
I follow you everywhere you go.
I watch out for you.
I protect your glow from ever leaving you.
And in return you wish to abandon me!
I can tell what you are thinking.
I can sense what you are feeling.

I am and will always be a part of you.
Don't think for one moment that you can forget that.
I am stricken by you.
Remember my name always.

Signed,

Your Shadow.

Life is not a sprint, it is a marathon. I have endured trials in almost every stage of my li
There has been many of moments where I cried out saying "why is this happening AGAIN!
You are never too old to stop learning. Even if a trial seems familiar, how you handled it
years ago will be different than how you will handle it today. The question you might want
ask instead of "why" is, "what". What can you learn this time? What are the trials' comm
theme? What lesson can you apply to your life so that you can close this chapter for goo
Switch the "w's" around so that your life can be changed around.

Your welcome.

Twisted but Not Broken.

"Yes, there is a small part of me that is twisted",
Stated by the anxiety.

"Yes, there is a small part of me that is crooked",
Caused by the trauma.

"Yes, there is a small part of me that begs for things to feel better",
Known by the grief.

"But there is the larger side of me that cannot nor will not be broken",

Accepted by the warrior.

I'll have to explain this one because the significance of 04 & 29 will not always be known. My mother was born on September 04th. My father was born on September 29th. When you put those two days together, you get 04-29, as in April 29th, as in my birthday. I'm pretty sure serendipity isn't the correct word to explain that numerical coincidence so if you know the correct terminology, please write me to shed light. Either way, I was not a coincidence. I was not a mistake. I was not adopted into a false pretense of reality. I am meant to be here in this moment, typing these words so that you can read these words and be inspired to keep going. Keep believing in yourself. Keep fixing your crown so you can one day wear it proudly. You got this.

04, 29.

04 x 29 = 116 different reasons
I gave myself that I am **enough**.

0.4% of 29 = 16 vantage points that
Revealed my manifested **destiny**.

04 divided by 29 = .13 seconds you have to get the
Fuck out of my face with your pathetic self.

04+ 29 = 33 years of polishing this
Delicately crafted porcelain doll who sits on her **throne**.

04 – 29 = 25 lonely years gone by
Hoping things will change.

September 04 and 29 united to birth **me**

Which by the way was not
A mistake!

*This is only the beginning. First step is to **HOPE** for more. I hope you will feel inspired to write. I hope you will feel ready to let go, walk away from that toxic relationship you obligated to stay in. I hope you achieve a richer and fuller life. One filled with love, admiration, success, and prosperity. I wish all this for you as I to, hoped the same for myse We will reach newer heights. We will persevere. We will overcome. Let's embrace our new beginnings.... Together.*

Pure Happiness.

The hard part about acceptance is
Getting past the reality that once
the emotions are in,
It becomes harder to deny they exists.

To accept pure happiness is to rid yourself of any
Doubt and uncertainty.
For me, pure happiness is utilizing my gifts to
Empower,
Inspire,
Unify,
Support,
You all.

I accept emotionality.
I choose to use it to connect with others.
I accept that my words may not be welcomed by everyone
However, that won't stop me from using them.
I renounce any negativity surround this project because
It was not easy to let myself be seen but, here I am.
I am meant to achieve greatness.
I will continue to be vulnerability as I
Navigate this thing called *life* in the
HOPE of impacting your life.

Thank You.

Made in the USA
Las Vegas, NV
18 February 2021

18117175R00035